Ponies

Kelley MacAulay & Bobbie Kalman

Photographs by Marc Crabtree

Crabtree Publishing Company

www.crabtreebooks.com

Ponies

A Bobbie Kalman Book

Dedicated by Julie Alguire
To my daughters Hayley and Lauren—in memory of Gingey Star

Editor-in-Chief
Bobbie Kalman

Writing team
Kelley MacAulay
Bobbie Kalman

Editors
Molly Aloian
Amanda Bishop
Kristina Lundblad
Kathryn Smithyman

Art director
Robert MacGregor

Design
Margaret Amy Reiach

Production coordinator
Katherine Kantor

Photo research
Crystal Foxton

Consultant
Dr. Michael A. Dutton, DVM, DABVP
Exotic and Bird Clinic of New Hampshire
www.ExoticAndBirdClinic.com

Special thanks to
Nancy Boudreau and Champy, Brooke Boudreau and Zoomer, Brittany Boudreau, Keith Makubuya, Emily Murphy, Candice Murphy, Leslie Brooks and Mac, and JL Equestrian Center

Photographs
All photographs by Marc Crabtree except:
Digital Stock: page 21 (water)
Comstock: page 21 (candy and lettuce)
PhotoDisc: page 21 (melon)

Illustrations
All illustrations by Margaret Amy Reiach except:
Katherine Kantor: page 18

Crabtree Publishing Company

www.crabtreebooks.com   1-800-387-7650

Copyright © **2005 CRABTREE PUBLISHING COMPANY**.
All rights reserved. No part of this publication may be reproduced, stored in a retrieval system or be transmitted in any form or by any means, electronic, mechanical, photocopying, recording, or otherwise, without the prior written permission of Crabtree Publishing Company. In Canada: We acknowledge the financial support of the Government of Canada through the Book Publishing Industry Development Program (BPIDP) for our publishing activities.

Cataloging-in-Publication Data
MacAulay, Kelley.
  Ponies / Kelley MacAulay & Bobbie Kalman ; photographs by Marc Crabtree.
      p. cm. -- (Pet care series)
  Includes index.
  ISBN 0-7787-1758-5 (RLB) -- ISBN 0-7787-1790-9 (pbk.)
  1. Ponies--Juvenile literature. I. Kalman, Bobbie II. Crabtree, Marc, ill. III. Title. IV. Series.
  SF315.M26 2004
  636.1'6--dc22
                                                    2004012799
                                                         LC

**Published in
the United States**
PMB16A
350 Fifth Ave.
Suite 3308
New York, NY
10118

**Published
in Canada**
616 Welland Ave.,
St. Catharines, Ontario,
Canada
L2M 5V6

**Published in the
United Kingdom**
73 Lime Walk
Headington
Oxford
OX3 7AD
United Kingdom

**Published
in Australia**
386 Mt. Alexander Rd.,
Ascot Vale (Melbourne)
VIC 3032

Contents

What are ponies?

Ponies are **mammals**. Mammals are animals that have backbones. All mammals have hair or fur on their bodies. A baby mammal drinks milk from its mother's body. Ponies belong to a group of mammals called the **equine family**. Horses, donkeys, and zebras also belong to the equine family.

A pony's body

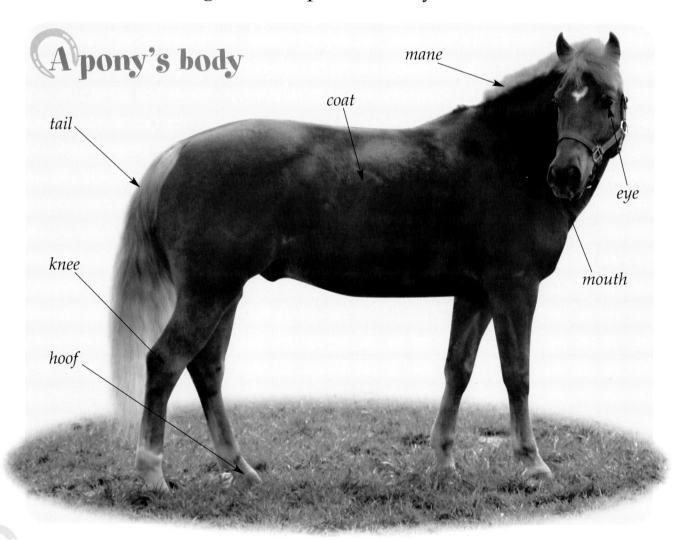

mane

coat

tail

eye

knee

mouth

hoof

Wild ponies

Long ago, many **wild ponies** lived in North America. Wild ponies are not owned by people. They live in groups called **herds**. The ponies in a herd always stay together. Today, there are few wild ponies left. Most ponies are **tame**. People must feed and care for tame ponies.

Like wild ponies, tame ponies do not like living alone.

Is a pony right for you?

Many children dream of owning a pony. Ponies are beautiful, friendly animals. Caring for a pony is a big responsibility, however! You will need to make sure your pony is fed, exercised, and **groomed**, or cleaned, every day.

Would you be a good pony owner?

Are you ready?

Before you decide to get a pony, discuss the following with your family.

- It is very expensive to buy and to care for a pony. Is your family prepared to pay for food, equipment, and special care?

- Ponies need a lot of exercise. Will you make sure your pony gets exercise every day?

- Who will feed your pony every day?

- Are you **allergic** to ponies?

- Are you willing to spend time every day with your pony?

- Where will you keep your pony?

- Ponies usually live for 20 to 30 years. Will you care for your pony for many years?

Plenty of ponies!

There are many **breeds**, or kinds, of ponies, but all ponies look similar. **Purebred** ponies have parents and grandparents that are the same breed. **Crossbred** ponies have parents and grandparents that are different breeds. Purebred ponies are more expensive to buy than are crossbred ponies. These pages show four popular pony breeds. The ponies you see in this book are a Pinto pony and a Haflinger pony.

The Pinto pony is usually a friendly breed of pony.

The Bashkir pony is famous for its curly coat!

Shetland ponies are usually calm and gentle.

The Haflinger is a popular pony breed from Austria.

Baby ponies

A baby pony is called a **foal**. A foal is born with all its fur. Unlike many other baby animals, a foal is able to see and hear when it is born. After a foal is born, it rests while its mother licks its body clean.

*A foal drinks milk from its mother's body for at least six months. When it is one month old, the foal also begins to eat solid foods, such as grass, hay, and **grains**.*

Shaky at first

A foal gains strength very quickly. It is able to stand up just a few hours after it is born! At first, the foal's legs are very shaky. After only one day, however, the foal can play, swim, groom itself, and even **gallop**, or run! The young foal still needs its mother's protection. The mother feeds and protects the foal for at least one year.

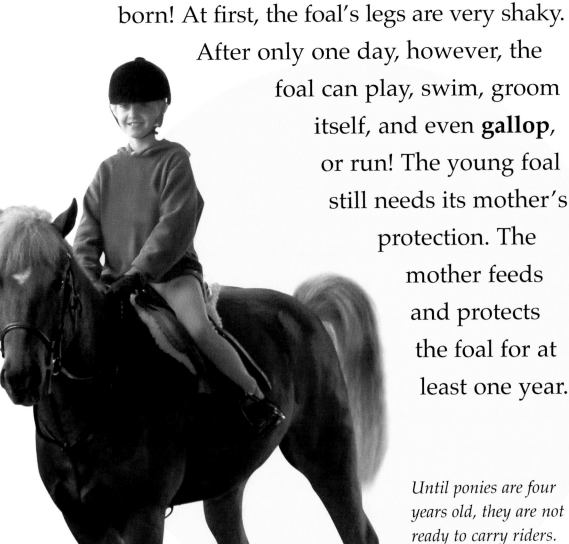

Until ponies are four years old, they are not ready to carry riders.

Picking your pony

Breeders are people who raise and sell ponies. You can buy a pony from a breeder, or you can ask your friends if they know anyone who is selling a pony.

Spend time with different ponies before you choose the one you want. Are you a very good rider? A good rider needs a lively pony. If you are just learning to ride, you might want to choose a calm pony.

What to look for

Take your time when you are picking the pony you want to own. Make sure you choose a healthy pony! A healthy pony has:

- a shiny coat with no bald patches.
- a sleek, strong body.
- clean eyes and ears.
- no trouble running.
- a clean nose and a clean bottom.
- no sores on its body.

Getting ready

In order to take proper care of your pony, you will need to buy a lot of special equipment. These pages show some of the things you will need to look after your pony properly.

A **halter** fits over your pony's head. You can use the halter to tie up your pony and to lead it around.

Your pony will need to eat different foods to be healthy.

A **haynet** provides your pony with plenty of fresh hay for eating.

A **dandy brush** removes dirt from your pony's coat.

A **body brush** smooths your pony's coat after it is cleaned.

A **curry comb** loosens dirt that is deep inside your pony's coat.

You will need a **hoof pick** to clean your pony's hooves.

Use a **sponge** to clean your pony's face.

A **salt lick** will give your pony the salt it needs in its diet.

The stable

Some ponies live in **stables**. A stable is a building where ponies and horses are sheltered and fed. The best stable for your pony may not be the one that is closest to your home. Visit several stables before you choose the one where your pony will live. Your pony's **stall** at the stable needs to be large and airy. The pony should be able to move around in the stall and lie down in it comfortably.

What to look for

Choosing the right stable for your pony is a big decision.
Below are some ways to know if a stable is right for your pony.

- The stalls are large and filled with fresh **bedding**.

- There is a full water bucket in each stall.

- The stalls have no sharp edges.

- The stalls are **mucked**, or cleaned out, every day.

- The ponies are exercised every day.

- The stable has a large field of fresh grass.

Try to visit your pony every day. If you visit your pony often, it will feel comfortable when you are there.

Living outdoors

If you own a large field, your pony can live outdoors. The field needs a strong fence around it so your pony cannot run away. Make sure the field has a lot of green grass for your pony to eat. Also check that there are no dangerous holes in the field in which a pony's leg could get caught. A shelter filled with fresh bedding will give your pony a comfortable place to rest.

Ponies do not like being alone. If your pony lives alone in a field, it may begin misbehaving. Try to keep your pony with another pony.

Daily care

You will need to do many jobs every day to care for a pony that lives outdoors. Outdoor ponies eat a lot of grass, but you should also bring your pony hay and packaged food to eat. Your pony will also need fresh drinking water every day. To be healthy, your pony must be clean. Groom your pony daily and muck out its shelter.

If your pony lives in a field, check on the pony twice a day.

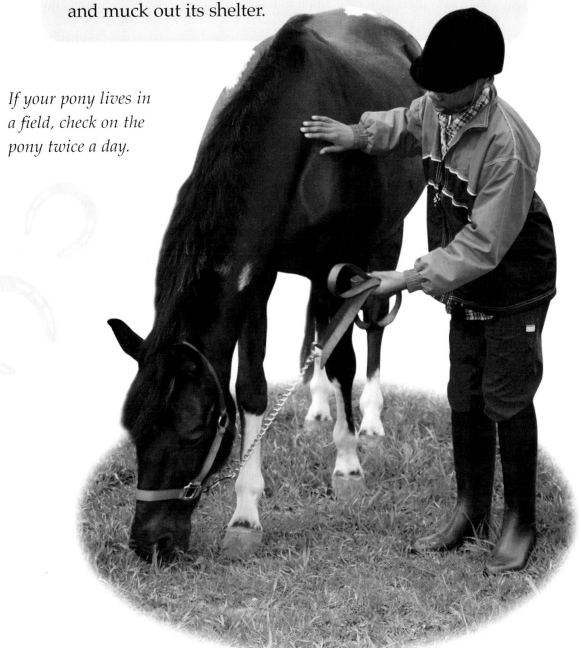

Pony food

To stay healthy, ponies need to eat a variety of foods. Your pony should always have plenty of fresh grass and hay to eat. You should also buy packaged food for your pony. Packaged food is a mixture of different grains and **minerals**. Ponies also need salt in their diet. If there is no salt in the packaged food, buy your pony a salt lick.

You can give your pony carrots and apples as treats.

Fresh water

Your pony should always have a large supply of fresh water to drink. Ponies need small drinks of water many times a day. If you give your pony water only once a day, it will take a big drink. Drinking too much water at once can make your pony sick.

Not on the menu

Be very careful which foods you give your pony. Some foods can make your pony ill!

- Candy and treats such as chocolate are not healthy for your pony.

- Fruits and vegetables that have not been rinsed properly may have harmful **pesticides** on them.

- Never give your pony spoiled foods. If your pony does not eat all its food in a day, be sure to take the old food away.

Grooming your pony

A pony needs your help to stay clean. Groom your pony every few days to keep it healthy. Your pony must be tied up when it is being groomed, so it will stay in one place. You may need an adult to help you groom your pony.

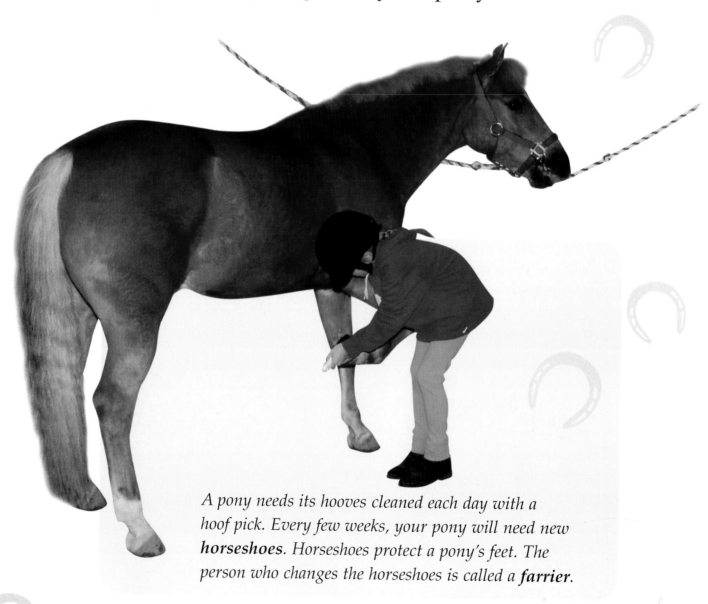

*A pony needs its hooves cleaned each day with a hoof pick. Every few weeks, your pony will need new **horseshoes**. Horseshoes protect a pony's feet. The person who changes the horseshoes is called a **farrier**.*

You must also keep your pony's coat clean. Rub a dandy brush briskly in the opposite direction to the way the pony's hair grows. Do not use the dandy brush on your pony's head or tail.

A curry comb removes any mud or sweat that is stuck in the pony's coat. Rub the curry comb in circles on the pony's body.

After cleaning the pony's coat, smooth the coat with a body brush.

Use a damp sponge to wash your pony's head. Do not forget to wash around the pony's eyes and nose! When you are finished, gently comb out your pony's mane and tail.

Pony exercise

Ponies have a lot of energy. They like to spend most of the day outdoors. Your pony needs at least one hour of exercise in an open space every day. It will not be healthy or happy if it never leaves its stall.

If your pony has been in its stall for a long time, it will be very happy to run around!

The best exercise

The best way to exercise your pony is to ride it every day. You must take lessons before you can ride your pony, however. Your instructor will tell you which equipment you will need for riding and how to put it on the pony. He or she will also teach you how to control your pony's movements. Remember that ponies are strong animals! You always need to be careful while riding.

Always wear a helmet and boots while riding your pony.

Understanding your pony

Ponies send messages to people and other animals. Watch how your pony moves its body. It may be trying to tell you something! These pages show some of the ways that ponies express themselves.

A pony that is rolling on the ground is scratching its back or just having fun! Rolling in the grass is a sign that your pony is happy.

A pony **paws**, or strikes, the ground with its hoof when it feels impatient or upset. If your pony paws the ground, it may want to go outdoors. Your pony may also paw the ground when it is hungry.

A scared pony kicks out its back legs or runs away quickly.

A pony that is angry will show its teeth.

Staying safe

A pony may bite if it is scared or hurt. To keep your pony relaxed and safe, follow the tips on these pages. If your pony should ever bite you, move away from it and allow it time to calm down.

Be careful not to pinch your pony while you are putting on its equipment.

Safety tips

Here are some important tips that will help you and your pony stay safe.

- Always approach your pony from the front. Walking up behind your pony and touching it may surprise and scare your pony.

- Ask your riding instructor to teach you how to lift your pony's hooves properly.

- Always begin petting your pony on its neck. Do not reach for its nose.

- Never hit your pony!

Always walk beside your pony when you lead it. Do not walk in front of the pony.

Visiting a vet

A **veterinarian** or "vet" is a medical doctor who treats animals. A vet makes sure your pony's body is in good condition. He or she also gives your pony **vaccines** with needles to keep it from becoming sick in the future. If you think your pony might be sick, call a vet right away.

A vet helps you keep your pony healthy.

When to get help

At the first sign of an illness, call a vet! Watch for signs such as:

- runny eyes or a runny nose.
- swollen ears.
- the pony eating less food.
- sores on the pony's body.
- the pony gaining or losing a lot of weight.
- the pony limping.
- the pony breathing quickly or slowly.

A great life

Caring for your pony means spending time with it every day. You need to feed the pony, groom it, and make sure it has a good home. Happy, healthy ponies live over 20 years. Enjoy all the time you have with your pony!

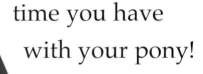

Words to know

Note: Boldfaced words that are defined in the book may not appear in the glossary.

allergic Describing someone who has a physical reaction, such as sneezing, to something

bedding Soft materials, such as straw or wood shavings, on which ponies sleep

farrier A person who changes a pony's horseshoes

grains The seeds of grasses such as oats and hay

horseshoes U-shaped pieces of metal that are nailed to the bottoms of a pony's hooves for protection

mineral A nutrient, such as iron or calcium, that humans and animals need to be healthy

pesticides Chemicals that are used to kill insects

stall A pony's living area in a stable

vaccine A medicine that helps protect the body from a disease

Index

1 2 3 4 5 6 7 8 9 0 Printed in the U.S.A. 4 3 2 1 0 9 8 7 6 5